A NIGHT
IN THE NABOKOV HOTEL

First published in 2006 by
Dedalus Press
13 Moyclare Road
Baldoyle
Dublin 13
Ireland

www.dedaluspress.com

ISBN 1 904556 55 8

Dedalus Press titles are represented in North America
by Syracuse University Press, Inc., 621 Skytop Road,
Suite 110, Syracuse, New York 13244, and in the UK by
Central Books, 99 Wallis Road, London E9 5LN

Typesetting and Design by Pat Boran
Cover image © Michael Boran

Printed and bound in the UK by Lightning Source,
6 Precedent Drive, Rooksley, Milton Keynes MK13 8PR, UK.

The Dedalus Press receives financial assistance from
An Chomhairle Ealaíon / The Arts Council, Ireland.

A NIGHT
IN THE NABOKOV HOTEL

20 Contemporary Poets from Russia

Translated and edited by

Anatoly Kudryavitsky

ACKNOWLEDGEMENTS

Grateful acknowledgement is made to the editors of the following in which a number of these poems, or versions of them, originally appeared:

The SHOp, Cyphers, Poetry Ireland Review, An Sionnach, Europski Glasnik (Zagreb), *Shadow of Time* by Anatoly Kudryavitsky (The Goldsmith Press, Ireland, 2005). Some of the poems in English translation were first broadcast on RTÉ Radio 1.

The author wishes to express his gratitude to Dr. Thomas Weber, OStR i HSO, of Goethe University, Frankfurt am Main, for his encouragement in the production of this bilingual volume.

in memory of

Gennady Aigi
1934 – 2006

Gennady Alexeyev
1932 – 1987

Igor Kholin
1920 – 1999

Victor Krivulin
1944 – 2001

Arvo Mets
1937 – 1997

Genrikh Sapgir
1928 – 1999

Contents

A Maple on the Outskirts of Town

how much silence
is hidden inside the tree
as if it's the only thing existing
in the whole wide world –
this quiet September maple!

o but there is much more to it –
like some kind of presence:
you stand before a door
you are calm and knowing:
the only important thing
is *in there*
and it is bigger than any concept

no need for explanation
but entry is possible
(departure—peace—oblivion)
at the cost of not seeing anymore
this quiet September maple

Дождь

и моросит и утихает
как будто возится сама с собой "случайность"

(как "одаренность" годная
лишь для набросков жалких)

как будто "есть" "живет"

(в кругу – как я – ненужности)

The Rain

drizzles and subsides
as if 'fortuity'
is romping with itself

(just as a 'talent'
capable only of middling sketches)

as if 'it exists' really exists

(in the circle of uselessness —
exactly where I find myself)

Метель в окне

В.Я.

Метель в окне и стены комнаты
и затеряв меня давно во вьюге дом
рисунков на стенах собрание как в прятках
как в юности – в ее далекой свежести
когда (метель) окно: как тайну: ладила
свое: то там то здесь:
немного поправляя

Snowstorm in My Window

For V.Y.

a snowstorm at my window
and these walls of my room—
my house lost sight of me in a blizzard long ago
the collection of drawings on the walls
playing hide-and-seek with me—
reminds me of how it used to be in my youth
in those days of freshness
when it (the snowstorm) decorated my window
building a mystery and going into details
adjusting every little thing:
now here, now there

Путь

Когда нас никто не любит
начинаем
любить матерей

Когда нам никто не пишет
вспоминаем
старых друзей

И слова произносим уже лишь потому
что молчанье нам страшно
а движенья опасны

В конце же – в случайных запущенных парках
плачем от жалких труб
жалких оркестров

Our Way

When nobody likes us
we learn
how to love our mothers

When nobody writes to us
we call to mind
old friends

And we utter a few words—simply because
we are scared of silence
and deem any movement dangerous

And in the end we find ourselves
in a park overgrown with shrubs—
and we sob as we hear the pitiable trumpets
of a pitiable brass band

* * *

пауза
которую я сделаю
прежде чем ответить
скажет вам больше

A Pause

if I pause
before I reply
to these words of yours
the moment
of silence
will be quite eloquent

* * *

люди писали
и в лагере
и в тюрьме
и в психушке
и где только не писали

главное
делать это незаметно

Writing

some people
would write in jail
in a labour camp
in an asylum

where have they not written!

the main thing is
to go unnoticed

* * *

когда я жду
я уже не жду
и как бы не нуждаюсь
дождаться

так и дожидаюсь

Waiting

when I am waiting
I am no longer waiting
I don't even need
to wait till it happens, indeed

now, isn't this the best way
to wait?

* * *

больше всего увидишь
если замрешь на одном месте
на зиму
    лето
    ночь
    день
как старый чемодан на балконе

Observation

you will see more
if you stand motionless
on the spot
for the whole winter
        summer
        night
        day—
like an old trunk
on the balcony

В начале весны

В начале весны
появляется потребность бедокурить:
щекотать
гранитных львов,
дразнить
гипсовых грифонов,
пугать
мраморных лошадей
и дергать за ногу
бронзового графа Орлова,
восседающего у ног
бронзовой Екатерины Второй.

В начале весны
возникает желание жить вечно —
но как осуществить
это безумное намеренье?

Спросил гранитных львов —
они не знают.
Спросил гипсовых грифонов —
они тоже не знают.
Спросил мраморных лошадей —
и они не знают.
Спросил бронзового графа —
он и понятия об этом не имеет.

Бронзовую императрицу
спросить не решился.

In Early Spring

In early spring
the tremendous temptation to make mischief:
      to tickle
granite lions,
      to tease
plaster gryphons,
      to frighten
marble horses
      and pull the leg of
the bronze Count Orlov,
sitting at the feet of
the bronze Catherine the Great.

In early spring
the new-born desire
to live forever—
      but how to realise such a goal?

I asked the granite lions
      but they wouldn't know.
I asked the plaster gryphons—
      they wouldn't know either.
I asked the marble horses –
      none had anything to say.
I asked the bronze Count Orlov—
      he hadn't the faintest idea
      about the whole thing.

I daren't ask
the bronze Empress.

Цветы

Цветы
пахнут похоронами
и любовью.
Но они
ни в чем не виноваты.
Иногда
ими осыпают негодяев,
иногда
их дарят круглым дурам,
иногда
их воруют на кладбище
и продают втридорога влюбленным.
Но цветы
ни в чем не виноваты.
Им не стыдно,
что Джордано Бруно
был сожжен на площади Цветов.

Flowers

Flowers
smell of funerals
and love.

It's not their fault.

Sometimes people
shower flowers
on rascals
or present them
to a silly bit of skirt.

Sometimes you see flowers
stolen from gravestones
and then sold
to pairs of sweethearts
at an exorbitant price.

It's not their fault.

Flowers are not embarrassed by the fact
that Giordano Bruno was burnt
on the Square of Flowers.

На нашей лестнице

Каждый вечер
на нашей лестнице
собиралась компания
молодых людей.
Они пили водку,
мочились на стенку
и хохотали над человечеством.
Каждое утро,
когда я шел на работу,
на лестнице валялась бутылка
и пахло мочой.
Как-то я сказал молодым людям:
Пейте на здоровье водку,
но не стоит мочиться на стенку —
это некрасиво,
а над человечеством
надо не смеяться,
а плакать.
С тех пор
на нашей лестнице
молодые люди пьют водку,
навзрыд плачут над человечеством
и изнемогают от желания
помочиться на стенку.
Изнемогают, но не мочатся.

In Our Stairwell

In the evenings,
a bunch of youths
dwelt in our stairwell.
They drank vodka,
pissed up the wall
and jeered humankind.
Every morning, as I went to work,
there was an empty bottle
on a landing,
and it smelt of urine.

Once I said to the youngsters,
'You may drink vodka if you wish,
but it would be better if you
refrained from urinating here,
it's not a nice thing to do.
As for humankind,
we should not laugh at it
but mourn it.'

Since that day
the youths in our stairwell
drink vodka,
lament bitterly over humankind
and exhaust themselves
abstaining from urination.
They would rather die than take a piss.

Радость

Вкушая радость,
будьте внимательны.
Радость, как лещ,
в ней много мелких костей.
Проглотив радость,
запейте ее
стаканом легкой прозрачной грусти,
это полезно для пищеварения.
Погрустив,
снова принимайтесь за радость.

Не ленитесь радоваться,
        радуйтесь почаще.
Не стесняйтесь радоваться,
        радуйтесь откровенно.
Не опасайтесь радоваться,
        радуйтесь бесстрашно.
И никого не слушайте,
        радуйтесь самостоятельно.

Глядя на вас,
и все возрадуются.

Beastmen

In the same old way
you get out of your beds
of your graves—
beastmen—
gather some food
rodents
vegetables
and take it all
back to your crypts

Inscriptions: signboards...

the genuine ones are
dissolved
in space
or in time
no tombstones
on their graves
none whatsoever

* * *

Тень
шорох тени
и нет хороших
в шорах
кто хорош?
рошхо рошхо!
Ни те, рох шо,
ни другие

Who's Good?

Shadows
rustling of shadows
and no good man
wears blinkers in the shade
who's good
goody-goofy-good?
Richard Roe, John Doe—
neither that shadow
nor the next

В скрипичном ключе

Рука подхвачена рукой
над нотой ля
октавы третьей.
Что слава сделала, другой
так не пометит.
То было время трудно-дней,
народного желанья славы.
Возможно ль выдумать людей
сложней, чем эти сплавы?
Терпением ожесточать –
какая стойкая привычка.
Разбей молчания печать,
скрипичный ключ, а не отмычка.

The Treble Clef

One hand is held up by another
over the A
of a high octave.
What glory has achieved,
cannot be tamed.
Those were the days of the Chief
Difficulties and the all-out search for fame.
Can you possibly imagine
people as complex as metallic alloys?
Their black magic
is their unchanging habit of embittering a man
by trying his patience.
If you want to break the seal of silence,
use the treble clef, not a picklock.

Новые сведения о Петрарке и Лауре

Лаура пишет письмо Петрарке
шрифтом Times New Roman
в интернет-тетрадке

письмо исчезает

Петрарка пишет сонет Лауре
пальцы бегут по клавиатуре

письмо исчезает

на платье Лауры осыпаются
букв лепестки

в этот миг
они так близки
что руку вот протяни
коснешься мизинца
левой руки

News of Petrarch and Laura

Laura types a letter to Petrarch
using the Times New Roman font

it's her blog

and it disappears

Petrarch types a sonnet for Laura
as an internal monologue
his fingers run restlessly along the keyboard

the sonnet disappears

the petals of syllables
fall onto Laura's frock

silence lingers
the two of them sit so close
he'd touch her little finger
should he stretch his right hand
into Cyberland

* * *

Я в осень вошел, как во взгляд,
как в тихий туман реки.
Зеленые тростники
качались зачем-то вдали...
Я в осень вошел, как в реку,
охваченную тишью снов.
И легионы слов
качались где-то вдали.
Я в осень вошел, как в слова,
потерянные кем-то вдали.

Autumn

I entered into autumn
as into somebody's glance,
or into a quiet mist on the river's face.
Green canes
were swaying in the distance.
I entered into autumn as into the river
embraced by the silence of dreams.
Myriads of words
were swaying in the distance.
I entered into autumn as into the words
someone had lost in the distance.

* * *

Преграда сна —
как ветер, рвущий в клочья
деревья гибкие.
Вчера — я снова жил.
Сегодня — только сплю;
проходит вереница
пустых мечтаний.
Волны ль это —
или песок — сыпучий, легкий и бесцветный?
Как будто дождь...

The Barrier of Sleep

The barrier of sleep—
is like the wind that rips these supple trees
to pieces.
Yesterday I lived again.
Today I'm only sleeping.
A row of empty dreams
passes before my eyes.
What is it that I see—
the waves?
Or maybe sand,
free-flowing, colourless and light?
It looks like rain…

* * *

Когда люди имеют мнения,
они обмениваются ими.
Когда люди не имеют мнений,
они обмениваются отсутствием мнений.

Opinions

When people have opinions,
they swap them.
When people have no opinions,
they swap the absence of opinions.

Эвридика

Пламя свечи виновато марьяжит.
Меняется форма, рождается шорох –
Орфея плач. Он слышит
удар руки по струнам звонкой лиры...
Связует нить воззрения паука,
повисшего над миром
мельчайших тканей, -
тянется за словом моим паутина –
златого дня немыслимый конец.

И пьет Орфей настой из терпких слов,
забывшись сном, над лирою склоняясь
и наблюдая гладь
сиреневого Стикса.

Eurydice

A candle flickers guiltily.
The flame changes its shape, and causes a rustle,
which is the weeping of Orpheus. He hears
his hand strike the strings of the resonant lyre...
The thread of thoughts of a spider
that hangs above the world
of fine-grained substance
is a cobweb trailing my words,
and this is the unthinkable end of the golden day.

And so Orpheus drinks an extract of bitter words,
which leaves him sunk into a reverie,
bent over the lyre and the glassy surface
of the lilac Styx.

* * *

Ночью:
серые мотыльки прячутся
в складках моей одежды.
Они наполняют мой костюм,
шелест их крыльев похож
на мой шепот.
А когда на улице
зажигают фонари,
они вместе летят на свет,
и костюм движется,
словно это я иду, скрывая лицо
под глубоко надвинутой шапкой,
но мои глаза – лишь рисунок на крыльях,
и душа моя – пыль.

Shades of Night

At night
grey moths hide themselves
in secret folds of my clothes.
They fill my suit.
The rustling of their wings sounds like
my whisper.

When all the street lamps
begin to shine
the moths fly up to them—
and it looks as if my suit is moving—
as though I walk hiding my face, my hat
pulled over my eyes.

But my eyes are
circles on butterflies' wings,
and my soul is dust.

*   *   *

Мне говорили:
—Полезные вещи нельзя на помойку,
полезные вещи еще пригодятся.
Мне подарили большую коробку:
в эту коробку поместится много
полезных вещей.
Мне нравится эта коробка,
она стоит улыбаясь,
в ней очень тепло и уютно
и я в ней легко умещаюсь,
а значит, я очень полезен
и, значит, еще пригожусь.

Not Rubbish

They used to say,
Don't scrap good things,
they will come in handy.
They presented me with a cardboard box
big enough to store
lots of good things in it…

I have a liking for this box
that stands here smiling.
It is big enough
to accommodate me.
I feel cosy in it,
I am warm.

Who knows, maybe this means that
I am a good thing
and will come in handy.

* * *

Рыбаки возвращаются без улова,
говорят:
—Река разлилась
и вода замутилась.

Рыбаки возвращаются без улова,
говорят:
—По реке идет грязь,
давно идет грязь, и рыбы уже не найдешь.
Но лишь высохнет наша одежда,
мы снова пойдем к реке.

Fishermen

Fishermen come back empty-handed.
Fishermen say,
The water is high,
the water is troubled.

Fishermen come back—
and spill and scatter like rain-drops.
Fishermen say,
Mud is floating down the river.
It's been long since it started,
and now the fish are gone.
But we shall return to the river
as soon as our clothes are dry.

*   *   *

Положи мои слова на землю,
утрамбуй их ногами, чтобы не поднимались,
чтобы сеточка подошвы отпечаталась на каждом,
чтобы никто их не трогал и,
проходя мимо, каждый говорил: «Бросовая вещь».
Чтобы их засыпало снегом,
чтобы на них мочились собаки,
чтобы они были незаметны словно
прошлогодние листья,
чтобы, глядя на них,
говорили: «Земля...»

Тогда подними мои слова к небу.

Words

Lay my words on the ground,
tread them down, ram them firmly,
so that the pattern of the sole leaves a mark on them,
and no one ever touches them,
and each passer-by mutters: "Such a useless thing"—
and snow covers them,
dogs urinate on them,
and they become indistinguishable
like rotten leaves,
and people, looking at them, say:
"That's clay."

Then raise them up to the sky.

Вариант

… Тогда сотворил Бог зеркало и отразился в нем.
Так Адам создан был, и Бог его любил как самого себя.
Дал Бог Адаму зеркало, посмотрелся Адам в зеркало –
так Ева явилась.
И любил ее Адам, как самого себя.
Посмотрелись Адам и Ева друг в друга, как в зеркало,
и появились у них дети,
и Ева любила их больше самой себя,
оттого дети любили только себя,
и убил Авель Каина.
В гневе разбил Бог зеркало и развеял по свету.
Оттого мы видим мир не как создал Бог,
но как отражает зеркальный прах.

An Apocryphal Story

…And God made a mirror, and the mirror
reflected Him. So Adam was created,
and God liked Adam as much as he liked himself.
God gave Adam the mirror. Adam looked at himself—
and Eve came into the world,
and Adam liked her as much as he liked himself.
Adam and Eve saw each other just as they
saw themselves in the mirror—
and unto them children were born,
and Eve loved them more than she loved herself.
Accordingly, the children loved nobody
but themselves—
and Abel rose against Cain his brother,
and slew him.
God was enraged;
he broke the mirror, and scattered its splinters.
And now we see the world not as it was made
but as reflected in grains of mirror sand…

Обрыв

Если обрыв не обрывается,
он не обрыв.
Радость его – обрываться,
на оползневых полозьях скользить.
Лепит статуи из глины обвал,
влажный глиняный язык
слизывает дома,
муравьиные люди в домах оглушенных
станут глиной сушеной.
Не растите, плоды,
растлевайте себя до рожденья,
торопите гниенье
на теле обрыва.
Это глинное море,
липкая сила –
веселье могилы.
Обреченный скитаться
среди глиняных статуй,
питаться
подаяньем бессмертия –
изнанки страха,
кто может без смеха
смотреть на смерть!

A Steep

If a steep isn't steep enough,
it's not a real steep.
Because it gives him pleasure
to be sheer and let landslides
slide down.
He moulds statues out of mud,
his wet loamy tongue
licks away buildings and huts.

Hey, ant men in your thunderstruck houses,
all of you will become
dry clay.
Fruits, don't grow,
deprave yourselves
before you have been conceived.
Hurry up your rotting,
you little sores on the body
of the steep.

Plunged into the sea of mud,
can you feel a sticky force,
the gaeity of the grave?
Doomed to wander amidst
mud statues,
to live by the charity
of immortality
and view the reverse side
of fear,
can you look at Death
without a laugh?

*   *   *

Жизнь сложена из лепестков розы
внутри которой развернут сад
где растет всего одна роза
размером с целый сад

ключ потерян

The Rose Garden

Life is formed of rose petals

there is a garden within that rose
and in the garden there is a single rose
as big as the whole garden

the key to the gate is lost

Царапина

карабкается по рукам,
царапает воздух шиповник,
вращает пращу аромата,
и падает голова губами в розовый зев.
Шиповник процарапал в воздухе дождь
и зигзаг — грозу,
губы вылепили розу,
влажную,
жадную,
махровую,
маслянистую,
математически четкую в очертаниях.
Кожа пружинит под нажимом шипа,
сок стекает на язык лепестка,
а лепесток языка
медленно следует вдоль царапины.
Царапины как бы Цезари,
перешедшие Рубикон,
шаг от простой страсти шиповника
в райскую фантасмагорию розы.

The Scratch

scrambles up the hands;
brier scratches the air,
swings the sling of fragrance—
and the head drops
into some pink throat, lips first.

Brier has scratched the rain
and the zigzag of lightning on the air.
Lips have shaped a double rose,
humid,
greedy,
oily,
mathematically precise in outline.

The skin is resilient
under the pressure of a thorn.
The juice streams down
onto the tongue of a petal,
and the petal of the tongue
slowly follows the scratch.

The scratch is Caesar,
who has just crossed the Rubicon,
a step from the simple passion of brier
to the heavenly phantasmagoria of a rose.

Компьютер любви

Небо – это ширина взгляда
Взгляд – это глубина неба

Боль – это прикосновение Бога
Бог – это прикосновение боли

Выдох – это глубина вдоха
Вдох – это высота выдоха

Свет – это голос тишины
Тишина – это голос света
Тьма – это крик сияния
Сияние – это тишина тьмы

Радуга – это радость света
Мысль – это немота души

Свет – это глубина знания
Знание – это высота света

Конь – это зверь пространства
Кошка – это зверь времени
Время – это пространство свернувшееся в клубок
Пространство – это развернутый конь

Computer of Love

The sky is the width of a look
A look is the depth of the sky

Pain is the touch of God
God is the touch of pain

Breathing out is the depth of inhalation
Breathing in is the height of exhalation

Light is the voice of silence
Silence is the voice of light
Darkness is the scream of shining
Shining is the silence of the dark

Rainbow is euphoria of sunlight
Thought is voicelessness of the soul

Light is the profundity of knowledge
Knowledge is the pinnacle of light

Horse is the beast of space
Cat is the beast of time

Time is space curled up into a ball
Space is the horse of extension

*   *   *

Молитва – это корабль
плывущий сквозь наготу
молитвенная луна
и солнце из поцелуя
молитва – это корабль
с младенцами на борту
когда он плывет в любовь
кормой океан целуя
Всемирная тишина
не может все заглушить
нам кажется что мы есть
и этого очень много
у Шивы есть много рук
но он не умеет шить
у Бога есть много ног
но наша любовь двунога
Двуногая нагота
распахнута в горизонт
и только корабль любви
плывет через Геллеспонт
живые давно мертвы
но медленно оживают

The Ship of Prayer

Prayer is a ship
that sails through bareness

the moon is prayerful
and the sun consists of kisses

prayer is a ship
with babies on board
she sails into love
kissing the ocean with her back

World-wide silence can't drown
worldly noises
we believe that we exist
and that life is in abundance
Shiva has many arms
but he can't bind sheaves
God has many legs
but love is bipedal

Two-legged nakedness
is wide open into the horizon
every lodging is temporal
only the ship of love
sails through Hellespont
time and again

the living have been dead for so long
but they are slowly now
returning to life

Крылья

Эти крылья –
справа – слева –
спереди – сзади –
это только одно крыло
преломленное
во всех пространствах
где нечетнокрылые
улетают
крыльями внутрь
здесь тайна твоя и моя
с нечетным количеством крыльев
В четырех измерениях души
сплетают
раковые уши.

Wings

These wings—
on the right—on the left—
in front—behind—
they are only one wing
refracted
in all dimensions
into which those with an odd number
fly away,
their wings turned inwards.
This is a secret, yours and mine,
a secret with an odd number of wings.
In some four-dimensional space
souls weave,
and perceive with,
such tentacles of lace.

*   *   *

Моему дому
Твоему знаку
Огненному столпу
творения
Голосом
не знающим боли
Отгородиться
и плакать
горько
Медленно
полыхая
ах я
уже
в хоре
но не тебе
и не мне
по кругу
каждому
свой вскрик
и невеста
Обворожительно
Преображенно
Нежно

Speaking for Yourself

To my home
To your sign
To the flame-coloured
pillar of creation—

speaking in the voice
oblivious of pain
shutting yourself off
from the world
and crying bitterly
blazing slowly:
ah, I joined
the chorus—

but it's not up to you
nor to me
to choose going round

to each one of us—
his own scream
or a dream
or a bride—
fascinating
transformed
gentle

Плач

Удивительная способность
Человека
Плакать
Вызывать жалость
Таким странным образом
Почему
Не плачут
Звери
Дома
Автомашины
Мне могут заметить
Что они тоже
Плачут
И что не всегда
Проливают слезы
От избытка чувств
Иногда просто
Соринка
Попала в глаз
Или что-то
Но я не об этом
Я о всемирном плаче
Когда содрогается
Вселенная
Когда все сливается
В единый
Вскрик
Вздох

Weeping

Isn't it amazing,
This human ability
To cry
To appeal for pity
In such a strange way?

Why animals
Don't cry
And houses
And cars?

Somebody may say
That they cry too
But seldom
Shed tears
Out of the fullness
Of the heart.

Sometimes
A speck of dust
Or something
Gets
Into somebody's eye
But this is not
What I'm talking about.

I want to tell you
About world-wide weeping
When the universe
Shudders
And everything merges
Into a single scream,
A deep-drawn sigh.

Из военного цикла

Командир батареи
Безусый
Парнишка
Рассматривал в бинокль
Поле
Утыканное
Ромашками
И васильками
Затем
Вдохнул
Полной грудью
Окопную вонь
Крикнул
Огооонь
И все полетело
Вверх тормашками

From *The War River*

The gun-commander
a young lad
wearing no moustache
used his field glasses
to examine the field

all about were dotted
daisies and cornflowers

the lad breathed in
the trench stink
and screamed:
Fire!

topsy-turvyness
the world is in a mess

* * *

Ни звезды
Ни креста
Ни черта
Волосы
Вместо травы
Торчат
Из земли
На братской могиле

.

Common Grave

No stars
No crosses
No nothing

Instead of grass
Hair
Sticks
Out of the ground
At the common grave

* * *

Э. Иодковскому

Если ты одинок,
Если тебе не с кем поговорить
Зайди
К самому себе
Поговори
Сам с собой

For Edmund Iodkovsky

If you are lonely
If you have no one
To talk to—

Why not
Visit
And try to talk
To yourself?

* * *

Одни говорят
Что я гений
Я говорю
Это
Действительно так
Другие говорят
Бездарен
Я подтверждаю
Третьи говорят
Я убил человека
Киваю головой
Все что говорят люди
Правда
Сотканная
Из пустоты

Truths

Some say
I am a man of genius
I never
Deny it
Others assert that
I am dull
I readily
Agree
Somebody alleges that
I murdered a man
I nod
Everything people say
Is a truth
Woven from
Emptiness

Рысь

золотоглазую мы не заметили Рысь
когда она следит не щурясь, не мигая
за солнцем, нет, за митингом:
сошлись
они стоят как тишина большая
защитники всего что ползает плывет
что ходит посуху и над землей летает...
но поздно уже... вечер... холодает
и, постояв, расходится народ

Lynx

that golden-eyed Lynx, we didn't notice it
as it watched the Sun,
oh no, it watched the meeting,
not even blinking…
they gather and stand still
like greater silence,
those protectors of everything that crawls, or swims,
or walks on dry land, or flies over…
but it is getting late… and growing cold…
and soon the people drift apart

Милые ошибки властей

эти милые сердцу ошибки властей
эти слабые волосы еле прикрывшие темя
розоватое!
это паренье частей
расчлененного Тела... и Небо стоит надо всеми
с выраженьем усталости, как бы заранье простив
что движения наши подобны растеньям
что назойлив простой эфемерный мотив
поражающий не превращеньем
но повторами
словно древнейший орнамент
искажает лицо:
это волчье, а то поросячье,
в лучшем случае — птичье...
подложный Эдем
перед нами разложен и властвует нами
и в глаза не глядит — но глаза по-животному прячет,
зарывая куда-то их, где хорошо и незряче:

где возможно прожить не увидясь ни с кем

Sweet Mistakes of the Authorities

o those mistakes of the authorities,
mistakes dear to our hearts!
this thin hair hardly covering the rosy
top of the head!
this soaring flight of the parts
of a dismembered Body...

the Sky hangs over us, showing signs
of fatigue, as if it has already excused us
for the vegetative way we move
and for that importunately simple, ephemeral motive,
subject to an amazing number of repetitions
but never to development –
just as an ancient ornament
distorts a face:
this one is wolfish, and that one pig-like,
or bird-like, at best...

counterfeit Eden
is displayed before us... it owns us
and never looks at us—but, like an animal,
directs its glance at some cosy blind spot

where one can live not seeing anyone at all

Пока мы изобретали рай

когда мы конструировали Запад
на сорока внутрисоветских языках
как некий Рай в золовых рукавах
как Ханаан, какой не занят
никем – и только нам обетован, –
мы видели египетские казни
вокруг себя, но жили безопасней
Обломова: схожденье на диван
святого духа с эмигрантским чтивом
портрет Набокова с пурпурною каймой...
когда ходил Господь по нищенским квартирам
и призывал на родину, домой –
в Европу, в Индию ли, в Палестину,
где Пуп Земли, а мы всегда не там...

While We Invented Paradise

while we constructed the West
in the forty Soviet languages,
just like some sort of paradise in our ashen hands,
or like Canaan, unoccupied and promised
to ourselves—
we saw the punishment of Egypt
but lived much safer than Oblomov[*]:
we would come down, the way the Holy Spirit did,
to a sofa, holding an emigré publication
and facing a portrait of Nabokov in the purple frame...

meanwhile, the Lord called on our beggarly abodes
and summoned us to our real homelands,
to Europe, or to India, sometimes to Palestine,
where the hub of the Universe can be found
but we are always missing...

[*]The hero of Ivan Goncharov's famous novel of the same
name (1858).

Книги и люди

худо, конечно, с какого конца ни возьми
но может быть, из-за того
полуослепшие книги тоже казались людьми
и скрывали преступное с ними родство

прятали а если за стенкой затихал сосед –
бережно – как шуршит папиросный слой! –
обнажали какой-нибудь порфироносный портрет
полоску с гольбеиновой Пьетой

Books and Men

indeed, it was bad from any point of view
but maybe because of that
weak-sighted books acquired a strange resemblance to people
and so had to conceal forbidden kinship

however, when a neighbour calmed down behind the wall
they would uncover cautiously—
the flimsy paper rustling timidly—
some regal portrait—or Holbein's *Pietà*

Над гранитной фабрикой

над гранитной фабричкой агатовая пыль
крошка ониксовая опаловая труха

тут тебе и творчество и лаборатория стиха
и традиции и национальный стиль
полудрагоценный камень превращается в утиль
в пепельницу или в тельце петуха

и полуслепой приемщицы ОТК
слабый штемпель
не смываемый
на века

Over the Granite Factory

in the air over the small granite factory, there are
hyalite crumbs, tiny bits of onyx and agathic dust

a classic example of a creative workshop
and poetic laboratory, a real booster
of traditions and the national style… semiprecious stone
turning into rubbish, like a figurin of a rooster
or an ash-tray—

and a quality inspector, a weak-sighted female,
stamps each object in the same way
with a pale mark,
never to be erased

Праздник продолжается

В общенародный праздник
ощущается
тепло толп
поглощающее

коллективное счастье
приглашает влиться
телесно

поднятые руки ищут напрасно
куда им деваться
кроме как на булыжники голов
сигаретный дым – с обыском
в карманы и бронхи
язык зрел и активен
но слова теряются
средь тысяч других слов

в праздник
снится всякое разное:
парад где молчащие мощи
влачатся по Красной площади
а ракеты присутствуют – наблюдательно –
на трибунах

проснешься –
праздник продолжается

пугая птиц
плавно восходят
огромные надувные человеческие лица

Festivities Go On

On public holidays
the warmth of the crowd holds you captive.
You merge into a vast mutual body.
Only your raised hands are free
but have nowhere to go
except down to the pebbles of heads.
Cigarette smoke searches
pockets and lungs.
Your tongue is almost autonomous
but your words get lost
among thousands of others.

If you doze off now
you will see anything in your dream,
even skeletons
marching past through Red Square
and rockets watching them
closely from the rostra.

When you open your eyes again
the festivities will go on.
You'll still have a chance to observe
the huge inflated faces
rising into the air.

Пограничный мыш

Он живет на ничейной земле.
Если граница проходит по реке,
он рыба, по болоту – лягушка.
Но все равно это пограничный
мыш, крот, бомж.

Он подсаживается в вагон
на глухой станции, роет ходы
в рюкзаках, саквояжах и кошельках,
затем спрыгивает из туалетной дырочки.
Не беспокойтесь за него, он не разобьется.

На каком наречии он говорит?
На языке "дай". Он разрывает сети слов,
как корни молодого деревца.
Его не поймаешь. Еще в древнем Урарту
он размежевал владения царя Обалдуя
и князя Удолбая. Его отменяли указами,
но он отменял издавших указы.
Более же всего отменял он
незнатных людей,
их плачевные жизни.
Будем справедливы:
он же и выкапывал им могилы,
правда, без опознавательных знаков.

The Border Mouse

He lives in no man's land.
If a boundary-line is drawn across a river,
he's a fish;
if it cuts through a bog,
he turns into a frog.
All the same he is
border mouse, mole, moss-trooper.

At stations he gets into carriages,
rummages through bags, trunks and purses,
jumps down through lavatory holes.
Don't worry about him,
he'll come to no harm.

Whether mouse or marmot, he speaks in
the language of Give-Me,
gnaws webs of words
like the roots of a sapling.
Although they have sought him
since the days of old Ur,
no one has caught him.

He demarcated the lands
of King Humpty-Dumpty
and Prince Dumpty-Humpty.
Annulled by edicts,
he annulled those who issued them,
though he more often annulled
very ordinary people, nibbling away at
their lamentable lives.
To do him justice, he dug
their graves for them.
The unmarked ones.

Бунин. Портрет с отсутствием объекта

В зеркале за его спиной плывет
вчерашний день
красные флаги и казачьи штандарты
его отражение –
полый силуэт

Кого-то втискивают
в оставленное им пространство
втискиваемый не помещается
кряхтит
потом устраивается как-то –

и трещит
каркас параллелей и меридианов

Bunin: Portrait with the Person Missing

In the mirror behind his back
recent times are floating
red flags and standards of the Cossacks
his reflection
a hollow silhouette

into the space he left
a man is being squeezed
he can't go in, groans
then somehow manages—

and the framework of parallels and meridians
cracks all over the globe

Псевдоалюминий и большие планы

Чем больше дом
тем меньше человек в нем живущий

то же с дьяволом —
вытеснял, бывало, хозяев из хибарки
в небоскребах же
умещается в табакерке

роль дьявола явно сходит на нет
его помет
однако
все еще густо лежит
на пустырях

студентов посылают
изучать эту красную глину —
высокой науки храм
учуял в ней псевдоалюминий
сырье для сверхбыстрых бомбардировщиков
и портретных рам

Pseudoaluminium and the Big Plans

The bigger the house,
the smaller the occupants.

The same goes for the devil:
in huts, he used to oust the inhabitants,
while in skyscrapers he can fit into a snuff-box.

The devil gradually loses prestige.
His dung, however, still lies in the fields.

They send students out
to investigate this red clay.
They hope, it contains much
pseudoaluminium,
the raw material of super-high-speed bombers
and portrait frames.

* * *

Внезапно сбежало лето.
—Янис Рицос

холодно-свинцовая масса
напоминает море

на набережной
два-три человека
в предвкушении солнца –
ощущении чуда

и я
вопросительным знаком
на шершавой скамейке

назойливо жду ответа

On the Quays

Summer suddenly fled.
—Iannis Ritsos

this cold leaden mass of water
bears some resemblance to the sea
as we know it

on the quays
are two or three men
waiting for the sun
feeling that miracles
may yet happen

I too am sitting there
on a flaking bench
looking like
an interrogation mark

I am waiting for some answer
determinedly

* * *

тихо так воет собачка
словно хочет повеситься
а не умеет

The Doggy

a doggy is whining—
oh, how quietly!
as if it wants to hang itself
but doesn't know how...

* * *

К.

хорошо выпить водки
в любую погоду
хорошо знать что время
кончается вместе со смертью
у меня еще есть в запасе завтра
которое пересекаешь ты

For K.

vodka is a treat
whatever the weather

it's nice to know
that time comes to an end
when we die

I still have tomorrow
to look forward to
and I know
you too will figure
in that fragment of eternity

Джеймс Джойс глазами советского читателя

читаешь в книге:
        дублин
        туман
        катафалк
        кладбище
отзывается сердце:
        москва
        кремль
        мавзолей
        владимир
        ильич

A Soviet Reader's Remark on James Joyce

you read in his book:
>	Dublin
>	fog
>	a hearse
>	a graveyard

your heart echoes:
>	Moscow
>	the Kremlin
>	the Mausoleum
>	Vladimir Ilyich

* * *

Поэт стоит в очереди за вермишелью.
Здесь же и его почитательницы.
Поэту немного стыдно.
Он стоял на эстраде,
словно маленький принц,
который никогда не ест.

The Poet

The poet stands in a queue
for spaghetti.

His female admirers
there too.

The poet is slightly ashamed:
he appeared on stage like a little prince
that didn't seem to need nourishment.

* * *

Исчезаю в весне,
в толпе,
в лужах,
в синеве.
И не ищите.
Мне так хорошо...

Absentee

I fade into spring
or into a crowd
or into a puddle

sometimes into the blue

there's no sense in looking for me:
I feel fine

* * *

Молодые девушки
похожи лицом
на небо,
на ветер,
на облака.
Потом из них получаются
верные жены,
лица которых похожи
на дома,
на мебель,
на хозяйственные сумки.
Но их дочери
вновь похожи лицом
на небо, ветер
и весенние ручейки.

Resemblance

Young girls
resemble in looks
the sky,
the wind,
the clouds above.

Later they make
devoted wives
whose faces remind us
of houses,
furniture,
carrier bags.

Still, their daughters
resemble in looks
the sky,
the wind
and streamlets in springtime.

* * *

Безденежный человек
ходит по городу.
Туманные звезды
дрожат на морозе.

Безденежный человек –
безрукий человек,
безногий человек,
безглазый человек.

В городе зажигаются огни,
и все видят –
у безденежного человека
голубые глаза.

Это не помогает.

Penniless Man

A penniless man
strolls about the streets.
Foggy stars tremble,
frost-bound.

A penniless man
is an armless man,
a legless man,
an eyeless man.

When all the city lights
begin to shine
everyone can see clearly that
the penniless man has got
blue eyes.

It doesn't help him.

* * *

Этот странный обычай
Присваивать людям имена
(или иногда номера)...
Без имени я уйду.
Без имени разве найдут.

Names

O that bizarre tradition
of giving people names
(or even numbers!)
Nameless, I will escape.
How can they possibly find
a nameless member of mankind?

* * *

Молчу
Молчи

Молчу
Молчи

Чутьем
Чутьем

Течем
Течем

Я думал
Мы о чем молчим

А мы молчали
Вот о чем

Untitled 1

I am silent
Keep silence

I am silent
Keep silence

By guess-work
By touch

We move on
We move further
But not much

I thought
We had hushed something up

But we
Hushed up
Even our chirruping

* * *

надо же
и тишина между нами
мальчиками и девочками

кусты
столбы   и луны
луны луны   ну
          не было войны

скажи ты

будто бы

а пусто было

не было
пусто

Untitled 2

picture this:
hushed silence dwells between us
between boys and girls

bushes
telegraph poles—and moons
many moons—as if
there were
no war

one could say

as though
there was
only void

there wasn't

*   *   *

Стой

Чувствуй

Гордись

куда денешься

вот теперь и гордись

столица

и столица гордится

вечным памятником
великим нашим
начальникам

как они стучали
на нас

каким большим большим
Кулаком

Pride

Stop

Feel

Be proud

you have no place to hide

so be proud now

capital city—

our capital is proud too

of the eternal monument
to our great leaders

how they banged
on their tables talking to us

banged on their tables with their big
BIG
Fists

*   *   *

вот кто
виноваты

разговоры разговоры
интеллигенты интеллигенты
чемберлены чемберлены
разгильдяи разгильдяи
инциденты инциденты
эпизоды эпизоды
экземпляры экземпляры
элементы элементы
симулянты
спекулянты
белофинны
контрабандисты
конкуренты конкуренты
интуристы интуристы
менделисты морганисты
формалисты
космополиты
мейерхольды мейерхольды
мандельштамы мандельштамы
буратины буратины
чебурашки чебурашки
интервенты интервенты
антиподы
оппоненты
супостаты
басурманы
виноваты
фантомасы
виноваты масоны

Who is to Blame?

They are
to blame:

talks, talks
eggheads, eggheads
Bohemians, Bohemians
incidents, incidents
episodes, episodes
specimens, specimens
elements, elements
simulators
speculators
Chamberlains, Chamberlains
White Guard
White Finns
smugglers, smugglers
rivals, rivals
foreign tourists
geneticists
formalists
cosmopolites
Meyerholds, Meyerholds
Mandelstams, Mandelstams
Fantomases, Fantomases
Pinocchi, Pinocchi
interventionists
invaders
antipodes
opponents
tyrants
infidels
all are to blame
freemasons
to blame

*   *   *

Все идиоты в этом мире идиотов
И каждый идиот идет отдельно

Все патриоты в этом мире идиотов
и каждый идиот идет отдельно

И каждый идиот по-каждому живет

В этом мире
в этом мире
каждый — идиот

The World of Idiots

How many idiots
in this world of idiots
and each idiot performing solo

how many patriots
in this world of idiots
and each idiot performing solo

and each idiot has an itch
to preach and teach

in this world
in this world
each idiot is
a figure of speech

Анти-новелла

Полное отсутствие действия

1. Никто ничего не делает
2. Никто нигде не находится
3. Никто ни к чему не стремится

Финал
Апофеоз тишины

Anti-Novella

Absolute absence of action

No one does anything
No one is present anywhere
No one seeks after anything

The grand finale
Triumph of stillness

* * *

Когда помру
я стану знаменитой
Я   знаменитой
                 знаменитой
   стану
   стану
Я стану
   стану
   стану
   стану   знаменитой
                              Ах
          знаменитой
          знаменитой
   стану
   стану

Foretaste

When I pop off
I shall be famous
          Famous
          famous
I shall be
I shall

                    I know

I shall
I shall
I shall be famous

                Ah

how   famous
          famous
          famous
I shall be

*   *   *

Россия с исснеженным зубром!
Твоей заповедной золы
я запах храню
для неубранных
для сладостно помнящих дым

Russia

O Russia, with its snow-covered aurochs!
I retain the smell of your sacred ashes
for those unharvested
for those delighted to remember
the sweetest fumes

Суд

Беседую как с другом,
С Богом.
Но верю лишь своим
Ногам.
Они несут меня, несут
На площадь –
На Великий Суд.
—Что случилось?
Кого собираются вешать?
Отвечайте же скорее!
—Говорят,
Казнят
Еврея.
Спрашиваю одного героя:
—Неужели всех
Врачей? –
(Смех.)
—Рабиновича?
—Рабиновича.
—А Гуревича?
—И Гуревича.
—И Петрова Ивана Петровича?
Покосился этот тип.
Холодный пот
Меня прошиб.
—Ты сам, случайно,
Не сектант?
Товарищи,
Интеллигент! –
Тут окончилась война,
И началась такая бойня,
Что даже Бог –

The Trial

I talk with God
as with a friend
but I only believe in my legs,
in the end.

They carry me,
they bring me
to the square.
The Last Judgement
is on there.

'What's happening?
Who are they going to hang?
Tell me!'

They say, they are
executing
Jews.

'Not all the medical men,
by any chance?'
I address a man of courage.

(Laughter.)

'Rabinovich?'
Rabinovich!
'Abramovich?'
Abramovich!
'And Gurevich?'
Surely, Gurevich!
'And Petrov Ivan Petrovich?'

Мой лучший друг –
Никого не уберег.

У Бога есть один дефект:
Его смущает интеллект.

The chap
looks at me askance.
I grow cold with fear.
You are not far
from a dissident, yeah?

Look, lads,
an egghead!

That instant the war came to its end
and the butchery began,
killings without remorse.
Even God, my best friend,
couldn't save anyone from the worst.

God has a critical defect:
he is perplexed by intellect.

Клевета

Напечатали в газете
О поэте.

Три миллиона прочитали эту
Клевету.
Незнакомцы,
Незнакомки
Шлют поэту
Анонимки:
—Спекулянт!
—Бандит!
—Убийца!
—Печать не может ошибаться!
—А еще интеллигент...

—Справедливые слова.
Общественность – она права. –
Сказали чукчи и эвенки.
Редактор на подал руки...
Друзья-интеллигенты
Поэту принесли венки
И траурные ленты.
А поэт пропал без вести.
Говорят,
Уехал в гости.
Ни покаяния,
Ни завещания,
На двери
Три
Буквы –
На прощание.

Lampoon

A paper published something
about a poet.

Three million people read that
slander.
Members of the public
started to thunder
against the poet.
They called him names
in poison-pen letters:
'Profiteer!'
'Bandit!'
'Murderer!'
'Papers don't make mistakes!'
'And he was regarded as an intellectual!'

'Public opinion can't be wrong.
Our anger is strong!'
Evenk and Chukchi peoples declared.
His publisher left him clutching air.
Fellow intellectuals shook his hand
and tendered him a wreath and a crepe band.

Meanwhile, the poet
left his place,
and disappeared without trace.
A rumour has it,
he went on a visit.
No repentance,
no messages left.
He simply put on his sweater,
wrote four letters,

На окраине Москвы
На шоссе
И в лесу
Поутру
По росе
Идет бандит и спекулянт:
Каждая росинка – чистый бриллиант!

Хорошо убийце
На зеленом лугу!
В солнце
Лес дымится
На другом берегу.
Посвистывает птица –
Газеты не боится.

beginning with 'f',
on his door—
and spat upon the floor.

Early in the morning,
'the bandit and profiteer'
walks along the motorway,
and passes through
a suburban grove.
Every drop of dew
shines like pure diamond.

'The murderer' feels fine here,
on these green meadows.
The forest on the other bank
steams in the sun.
Birds whistle,
and hares caper—
they are not afraid of the paper!

Зло

в младенце сидело
Зло

оно сжимало
пухлые нежные кулачки
топотало
розовыми ножками
(все в перевязочках)
рот –
шире лица:
дай!
земля намазана небом –
толстый пирог
ешь – не хочу!..

но когда оставались
последние крохи
старик взвыл:
Боже мой! Боже!
меня сожрало
Зло

Evil

inside the baby
Evil was hiding

Evil clenched its
plump and tender fists
Evil tramped the floor
with its tiny pink feet
(all bandaged up)

out of Evil's mouth
as broad as its face:
give me this!
give me that!
the land was spread
with skies
like a thick pie:
appease your appetite!..

with only a few crumbles left
the old man
screamed:
Oh, my God!
Evil
has gobbled me up!

*   *   *

Тс-с
Слышите

И еще

И это

И там

И далеко-далеко

Sounds of Silence

Hark, hearer
can you hear it?

And this

And again

And there

And far, far away

Умирающий Адонис

Я – Адонис
Я хромаю и кровь течет из бедра
Я корчусь – червяк на ладони
Не отворачивайся Природа будь добра
Я – сын твой Адонис

Меня погубила дура из бара
Обступили какие-то хмуро и серо
Я падаю – мне не дожить до утра
Мне дурно

Вот приближается рокот мотора
Меня освещает белая фара
—Как твое имя парень?
—Адонис
"Адонис? Латыш наверно или эстонец"

Я – Адонис
Я совсем из другого мира
Там апельсины роняет Флора
Там ожидает меня Венера
И о несчастье узнает скоро
Дикие вепри
Бродят на Кипре...

—Ах ты бедняжка!
"Понял! он – итальяшка"

Я – Адонис!
Я чужой этим улицам и магазинам
Я чужой этим людям и трезвым и пьяным
Поездам телевизорам телефонам
Сигаретам газетам рассветам туманам

Dying Adonis

I am Adonis
I am limping, my thighs are bleeding
I writhe like a worm
On somebody's palm

Mother Nature, I beg thee
Don't turn your back on me
I am your son Adonis

A stupid barmaid ruined me
Some gloomy figures beset me
I am fainting, I am dying on my feet
I won't live to hear sweet morning birds…

Suddenly—roaring of a motor
A shaft of light
'What's you name, lad?'
'Adonis'
'Adonis? Must be Latvian or Estonian'

I am Adonis
I came from a different world
Flora drops slow oranges there
Venus is waiting for me
And will soon learn of my misfortune
Wild boars are roaming
In Cyprus…

'Poor thing!
He's from Italy, I think.'

I am Adonis
I am a stranger to these streets and shops

"Нет
Скорей
Это
Еврей"

Я – Адонис
Я сквозь дебри за вепрем бежал и дрожал
Меня ветки за пятки хватали пытали
Меня били! любили! хотели! потели!
Я любезен богине Венере
Я не здесь! Я не ваш! Я не верю!

—Сумасшедший ясно
—Но откуда он?
—Неизвестно

Я – Адонис

These telephones TV sets and bus stops
Cigarettes newspapers dawns and fogs
I have nothing in common with those folks…

'He sounds
like a Jew'
'He *is* one
I tell you'

I am Adonis
I was forcing my way through thickets
I was chasing a wild boar
Branches grasped me by my heels
I was sweating I was beaten
I was loved I was wanted
Venus is fond of me
I don't belong here
I am not one of you
Believe me, it's true…

'A half-wit, surely'
'But where does he come from?'
'No one knows.'

I am Adonis

*   *   *

Доведены до нервного тика,
тикают тихо отовсюду часы.
Я переворачиваю,
переворачиваю их циферблатами вниз.
Я не верю во время.
Что это?
Упорядочение и упрощение.
Времени нет
(у меня нет времени) —
есть временнóе пространство,
врéменное, пока
ходят часы.
Переверните их циферблатами вниз —
и будем жить вечно —
будем жить вечностью.

Clocks

Driven to tic and tick-tock,
clocks are ticking everywhere.
I turn them over, one by one,
faces down.
I don't believe in time.
What is this word supposed to mean?
Surely, nothing else but
regulation, simplification.
Time is no more
(and I have no more time.)
Whatever still exists is infinite space,
aka temporal space: it will cease to be
when all the clocks stop.
Turn them over, faces down—
and let us live forever,
live by eternity.

*   *   *

Разве башня из камня
властна над ветром,
поселившимся в ней?
Это он колышет ее изнутри,
очертанья меняет.
Так и тело.
Так и душа.

The Tower

Does this stone tower
have power over the wind
dwelling therein?
No, it is the wind that sways it from inside,
changes its shape.

Behold, the soul –
and its bodily stronghold.

*   *   *

Город влажный лежал под нами –
купола раскрытых зонтов, закрытых, шпили –
куполов бокалы, шпилей фужеры –
мужчина и женщина –
вожделенный, желанный город.
Только крыши тонкая жесть,
только боль
между нами,
между нами и небом.

The City

The damp city rests beneath us—
domed umbrellas, spear-shaped umbrellas,
broach-spires, cup-like domes, goblet-like domes.
A man and a woman—
and a city,
the desired, beloved city.
Between us
only the thin tin plates of this roof
and the pain.
Only the pain between you and me.
Between the two of us and the sky.

*   *   *

Спит-сопит общий вагон
скорого.
Скрючились люди, изогнулись до боли,
конечности затекли,
позвоночники ломит,
неспособные тело держать.
Извиваясь, ползут по Земле
ожелезневшие голые
останки ящеров древних –
позвоночники-поезда.
Неподвижно лежат
позвонки-вокзалы –
мощный хребет планеты.
Только ты, поэт,
беспозвоночный, бескостный,
любую форму принять способен –
и бесконечного –
в Млечный Путь,
в железную дорогу –
хребта всех вселенных,
и обрастать
плотью жизни.

Long-Distance Train

A sleepy-wheezy
hard-seated carriage.
People huddled together,
their limbs become numb,
their backs aching,
their spines unable to hold their bodies up.

Iron skeletons of trains
crawl upon the surface of the earth,
ugly as they are,
wriggling,
resembling the remains of ancient pangolins.
Vertebrae of stations
are motionless –
the mighty backbone of our planet.

Only you, poet,
you spineless, boneless creature,
can take the form of everything,
including the infinite.
Cannot you turn into Milky Way
or become a railway,
the backbone of the universe—
and then attain the flesh
of the everyday?

*   *   *

Ночью, в Набоков-отеле
            школьницу, полую Лолу
В номер на птицу-постель
            змей-господин завлечет
Змей о семи головах:
            первая жрет насекомых
Гонгорой бредит вторая
Третья целует в пупок
            в полудетские груди Лолиту
Зверь о семи головах
Веки закрыла седьмая:
            молится Богу впотьмах

In the Nabokov Hotel

At night, in the Nabokov Hotel
      Sir Serpent entices
A schoolgirl, the hollow Lola,
Into his room
      and onto his bird-shaped bed.
Seven-headed Sir Serpent.
      The first head gorges itself on insects,
The second is mad about Gongora,
The third kisses Lolita on her navel
      and childish breasts.
Seven-headed Sir Beast.
The last head has weighed its eyelids down
      to pray to some God in the dark.

Акула-кунсткамера

Вот акула-кунсткамера. В ней
Головы турок в спирту
Петр в железных ботфортах
Церберша ангальт-цербская:
        в ноздрях сияют алмазы
В заднице блещет топаз
Рядом кленовый Пахом,
        ладан, церковное пенье
Пушкин на девке верхом,
        пишущий стихотворенье
Дивно бродить и смотреть
В многокамерной рыбе, правдивой как смерть.

A Shark as a Cabinet of Curiosities

Inside a shark there is a cabinet of curiosities.
Watch these heads of Turks
                    preserved in alcohol,
Tzar Peter in his iron jackboots,
The Cerberus of Anhalt-Zerbst,
                    diamonds shining in her nostrils
And a topaz sparkling in her arse-hole.
The maple Pakhom sits beside her.
                    It smells of incense,
A choir is singing.
Pushkin is also here
Positioned on top of a whore
                    and writing a poem.
I do like to stroll through these rooms
looking round and holding my breath
In this spacious fish, truthful as death.

Левиафан

Чешуеглазый,
         с дрожащим Ионой во чреве
В недрах узилища рыбного,
            в тесноте кровокамеры хищной
Страшно и нечем дышать
            в государстве его биоклеток
В социуме телец
            кровяных
                     под командой турбинного мозга.
Скоро ль извегнешь назад
            поглощенных, заглоченных толпы?
Скоро ль нырнешь без возврата
            вниз, на библейское дно?

Leviathan

Scaly-eyed,
      it harbours trembling Jonah in its belly,
In the bowels of its fishy dungeon.
      How scary it must be – choking in the cramped
Blood-coloured chamber
      of some predatory cellulate republic,
Suffocating in the community of blood corpuscles
      under the command of a turbine brain!

When will you disgorge what you have swallowed,
      those countless multitudes?
When will you dive back
      to the scriptural depths, forever?

Башня-библиотека

Башня до самого неба,
              башня-библиотека
Вьющихся лестниц извивы,
              фолианты в размер этажей
Хмель-виноградьем увитые
              с заржавленными замками
На шумерских цепях
Здесь чернокнижье цветущее –
              тайную мудрость Адама
Кто-то постигнет, вместит,
              и тогда остановится время
Ангел свернет небеса

The Library Tower

It's a library tower,
　　　　and it pierces the sky.
Hop and vine
　　　　twine around
Winding stairs
　　　　and storey-sized volumes.
All the locks on Sumerian chains
　　　　are rusting.
Black magic is blooming here,
　　　　the secret wisdom of Adam.
Some day somebody will apprehend
　　　　and master it—
And time will come to a halt,
An angel will furl the sky.

Собака Павлова-1

Аленушка Васнецова
в концентрационном лагере.
Плачет.
Разлука с братом.
Я не хочу быть человеком.
Я хочу быть автоматом.

Писатель, расстреливающий читателя,
получает Нобелевскую премию,
последнюю в мире.
Полноценное творчество –
это отсутствие конкурентов.
Мир пуст.
Гениальность. Гениальность. Гениальность.
Пусть.

Одиночество.
Индивидуализм.

Аленушка в концентрационном лагере,
поговорим?

Pavlov's Dog 1

Vasnetsov's Alyonushka[*]
in a concentration camp.
Crying.
Separated from her brother.
Don't wanna be a man,
wanna be an automaton.

A writer shoots his reader
and receives the Nobel Prize,
the ultimate one.
Perfect creation is the absence
of rivals.
The world seems empty now.
Talent. Talent. Talent.
And then?

Individualism.
The loneliness of a hawk.

Alyonushka in a concentration camp,
let's talk?

[*]An allusion to the famous painting *Sister Alyonushka
and Brother Ivanushka* by Viktor Vasnetsov.

Собака Павлова-2

Считалось, что нужно
вымыть руки, вытереть
махровым полотенцем, закончить
школу, различать
мужчину и женщину, основные направления
современной
философии,
вести учет
бумагам, ежегодно
обследоваться в районной
поликлинике,
похоронить мать, дерево вырастить, сына
считаться отцом,
знать уголовный кодекс, *врага в лицо –*
зачем? Если можно стрелять ему в спину.

Pavlov's Dog 2

They say, one must
wash his hands and then dry them
with a Turkish towel,
go to school,
be able to tell
a man from a woman,
be acquainted with popular trends
in modern philosophy,
register incoming papers,
have regular check-ups
at the local doctor's,
bury his mother,
plant a tree,
be regarded as his son's father,
know the criminal code,
know his enemy by sight—
but what for? *One may just as well
shoot him in the back.*

Собака Павлова-3

La Scala
Собака Павлова пела
груди кулонов вздымая:
«ла-ла-ла»

Публика
улетела
пробуя
в опере
возвышенно умереть.
Но Павлова пела
также как пила и плевала
(а этим животности не преодолеть).

Собака Павлова пела.
Люди выли из зала,
нутрь вылизав зря —
грязь вылезала.
«Ла-ла-ла» —
арию подвывали
«ла-ла-ла»
арию зла?

Pavlov's Dog 3

La Scala.
Pavlov's Dog was singing,
raising pendants on her breasts:
La-la-la.

The audience
was flying
high,
trying
to die
gracefully
as in any good opera.
And Pavlova was singing
as naturally as she would drink
or spit
(but in so doing
she couldn't overcome the brute.)

Pavlov's Dog was singing.
Members of the public screamed,
licking clean their insides.
All in vain:
the filth was overflowing.

La-la-la,
they echoed,
la-la-la—
joining in an aria of Evil—
along with the devil?

Ева Браунинг

Где ты
Ева Браунинг
мглистая девочка зверств
Лолиточка пистолетов
ласковых окупаций

корявая куколка смерти
муза расовых чисток
пациентка конца
любовница абсолюта

Где ты
Ева Браунинг
мудрая бабочка Вагнера
муть арийского хаоса
Русская мать насилия?

Eva Browning

Where are you
Eva Browning
brutality's misty girl
Little Lolita of pistols
and tender annexations

crooked chrysalis of death
Muse of ethnic cleansing
private patient
of The End
concubine of the absolute?

where are you
Eva Browning
Wagner's wise butterfly
residue of Aryan chaos
the mother of Russian violence?

Biographical Notes

Gennady Aigi (1934—2006) was born in the Chuvash Republic, and lived in Moscow. His translations of French poetry into the Chuvash language brought him recognition at the beginning of his career as a writer. However his unusual work wasn't welcomed in Russian periodicals and publishing houses. After *perestroyka* he published many critically-acclaimed books of his poetry in Russian and Chuvash, as well as numerous essays and translations. His poems were translated into many languages. Without exaggeration, he was the most celebrated Russian poet of his time. A book of his poems in French translation, entitled *Veronica's Notebook,* was published in Paris in 1984. Peter France of Edinburgh published two books of his translations into English, which were widely praised. Aigi was awarded the Golden Wreath of Struga (Macedonia), the French Academy Translators' Award and the Andrey Belyi Prize for Poetry (1987). In 2000, he was awarded the first-ever Boris Paternak Prize for Poetry.

Ivan Akhmetiev was born in Moscow in 1950. He started writing at the end of 1960s. Until 1989 only one of his poems was published in Russia. Since then many of his poems have appeared in literary magazines in Russia and abroad. Critics defined him as a minimalist and miniaturist. His collection of poems entitled *Poems, only Poems* was published in 1993. Some of his miniatures have been translated into German and English.

Gennady Alexeyev (1932—1987) lived in St. Petersburg, and lectured on History of Art at St. Petersburg University. He was the first to introduce *vers libre* (free-verse) in St. Petersburg. Writing in that style as early as in 1953, he published his first poem in 1962, but afterwards had difficulties in publishing his poetry which was regarded as 'different'. During his life-time, four collections of his poems appeared in Russia. Two more were published after his death, the latest one being *Me and the City (1991)*. Two volumes of his *Collected Poems* are due from a St. Petersburg publisher in the near future. Undoubtedly, he was one of the most important St. Petersburg poets of the second half of the last century; arguably, the most underestimated.

Vladimir Aristov was born in 1950 in Moscow, where he still lives. Educated at Moscow Institute of Technology and Physics, he started writing poetry at the end of 1970s. He was a member of the so-called *Poetry Club* circle, which included predominantly ironic poets. His poems, essays and short stories remained unpublished until the years of *Perestroyka*. Since then five critically-acclaimed collections of his poetry, including *Moving Away from this Winter (1992)* and *Private Follies of Things (1997)*, have appeared in Russia. His short stories were published in *Zhuzhukiny Deti,* the anthology of Russian short stories and prose miniatures written in the second half of the last century. His work has been translated into several European languages.

Sergey Biryukov was born in 1950 in Tambov. Having lived in Moscow, he is currently based in Halle, Germany. He started writing poetry at the end of 1960s, and saw his first poem published in a literary magazine only in 1989. Since then, he has published four collections of his poems; the first of them *The Muse of Zaum (1980)* is regarded as the most important. He has also published the monograph entitled *Zevgma: Russian Poetry, Mannerism to Postmodernism (1994)*, as well as a number of books on the history and theoretical aspects of Russian avant-garde. He was the founder and President of the Academy of Zaum, which includes Futurist poets from all over Russia. His work was translated into several European languages. He won the first prize at the Berlin International Poetry Competition, and was the recipient of the Alexey Kruchenykh Poetry Award. He has read from his work at several international poetry festivals.

Vladimir Earle (pen name of Vladimir Gorbunov) was born in St. Petersburg in 1947. Having worked as a fireman, a laboratory assistant and as a watchman, he is now a librarian. He started writing poetry in 1962 as a 15-year-old. In a few years he became a member of the so-called *Helenooct* group of young poets that existed between 1966 and 1971. His poems were widely published in *Samizdat* and in the Western Russian-language magazines. Since the years of *Perestroyka* he has published three critically-acclaimed collections of his rather experimental poetry, *Helenooctism (1993)*, *The Grass, the Grass (1995)* and *In Search of the Lost Xeif (1999)*, as well as many essays on the Russian literature of the 20th century. Among the authors he has translated into Russian are Samuel Beckett and Franz Kafka. He was awarded the Andrey Belyi Prize for Poetry (1986) and the David Burliuk Prize for Futurist Poetry (1991).

Dmitri Grigoriev was born in 1960 in St. Petersburg where he still lives. A graduate of Leningrad State University, he travelled the world extensively, and wrote poetry. However he wasn't allowed to publish anything until *Perestroyka*. Some of his poems, though, did find their way onto the pages of a few American Russian-language magazines. At the beginning of the 1990s three collections of his poems appeared in St. Petersburg. He is now regarded as one of the most important St. Petersburg poets of his generation. A volume of his *Selected Unpublished Poems* came out in 1992. Since then, he has published three novels and four collections of poetry, including *Crossroads (1995)* and *Fiery Yard-Keeper (2005)*.

Elena Katsuba was born in 1946 in Kamensk near Rostov, and educated at Kazan State University. She has lived in Moscow for many years, working as a journalist. Her first poem was published in 1963, after which her poems and short stories appeared only in unofficial periodicals in Russia *(samizdat)* and abroad. Since 1999, she has published three collections of poems, including *eR-eL (2002)* and *Igr Rai (2003)*, and also a dictionary of palindromes. She was the founding member of the *DOOS* group of poets (with Konstantin Kedrov). *http://metapoetry.narod.ru*

Konstantin Kedrov was born in 1942 in Moscow, and was educated at Moscow University. Poet, essayist and philosopher, he started writing poetry at the end of 1950s. In 1984 he founded the *DOOS* group of poets (with Elena Katsuba). He is editor of the Moscow-based *Zhurnal Poetov/Poets' Magazine.* Since the beginning of *Perestroyka* he has published 6 collections of his poems, including *Computer of Love (1990), Vroutselet (1993), The Gamut of Hamlet's Bodies (1994), Ulysses and Navsikaya (1997)* and *Sam ist Dat (2003).* A volume of his *Collected Poems* entitled *Or* appeared in Moscow in 2002. He has also published three books of his essays on literature and philosophy, including *Poetic Cosmos (1989).* He is the current President of the Russian Poetry Society. In 2003 and in 2006, he was the recipient of the GRAMMY.ru Poet of the Year Award.
http://metapoetry.narod.ru

Igor Kholin (1920—1999) was born and lived in Moscow. In his youth, he was employed as a waiter, then joined the Russian Army, took part in the World War 2, was wounded, and retired when the war ended. At the beginning of 1950s he became a member of the now famous *Lianosovo* group of poets and painters. Under the Communists, his poems appeared only in émigré magazines, such as *Strelets/The Archer* and *Tretya Volna/Third Wave.* In 1989, the first book of his poems, entitled *Poems with Dedications,* was published in Paris, in Russian, and subsequently reprinted in Moscow. His next collection appeared in 1995. At the end of 1990s, he published a number of his short stories. After his death in 1999, a large volume of his *Collected Poems* appeared in Moscow, followed by another large volume, this time of his *Collected Stories.*

Victor Krivulin (1944—2001) was born in Krasnodon, in the Ukraine. From 1947 he lived in St. Petersburg. He was educated at Leningrad State University, where he studied Russian and Italian literature. In the 1970s, he was closely associated with two of the Russian *samizdat* magazines, *37* and *Severnaya Pochta/Northern Post,* where he published his poems and essays. He belonged to the so-called *New Leningrad school of poetry,* which also included Joseph

Brodsky, Elena Shvarts and Sergey Stratanovsky. After *Perestroika*, he became involved in politics, and was at the head of the St. Petersburg branch of Democratic Russia, the pro-democracy political party. Among his critically-acclaimed collections are *A Concert of Requests (1993), Borderland (1994), Bathing in Jordan (1998)* and *Poems of the Jubilee Year (2001)*. His poems were translated into many European languages. In 1978, he was awarded the first-ever Andrey Belyi Prize for Poetry.

Anatoly Kudryavitsky (pen name of Anthony Kudryavitsky) was born in 1954 in Moscow of a Polish father and half-Irish mother. Having lived in Russia and Germany, he now lives in Dublin. Educated at Moscow Medical University, he later studied Irish history and cultural heritage. In the following years he worked as a researcher in immunology, as a journalist and as a literary translator. He started writing poetry in 1978, but under the Communists was not permitted to publish his work openly. Since 1989 he has published a number of short stories, seven collections of his Russian poems, the most recent being *Graffiti (1998)* and *Visitors' Book (2001)*, and a book of his English poems entitled *Shadow of Time* (Goldsmith Press, Ireland, *2005*). His poems and short stories have been translated into nine languages. In the 1990s he edited *Strelets/The Archer* literary magazine, an anthology of new Russian poetry entitled *Poetry of Silence (1998)*, and *Zhuzhukiny Deti (2000)*, an anthology of Russian short stories and prose miniatures written in the second half of the 20th century. He was the founder and first President of the Russian Poetry Society. In 2003 he received the Edgeworth Prize for poetry, and in 2005 was shortlisted for the Robert Graves Poetry Award.
http://uk.geocities.com/akudryavitsky

Alexander Makarov-Krotkov (pen name of Alexander Makarov) was born in 1959 in Tyumen. He now lives in Moscow and works as a journalist. He started writing poetry in the 1980s, and his first poem appeared in a literary magazine in 1989. Since then, he has published three collections of his poetry miniatures; the two most recent are *Deserter (1995)* and *Nevertheless (2002)*. He has read from his poems at literary festivals in Germany and Italy. His work has been translated into several European languages, and he was awarded the Grand Prix at the International Poetry Festival in Salerno, Italy (1992).

Arvo Mets (1937—1997) was born in Estonia, and educated at St. Petersburg University and at the Literary Institute in Moscow. He lived most of his life in Moscow where he edited several literary magazines, including *Novy Mir/New World*. He started writing poetry in the early 1960s, and also translated Estonian poetry into Russian. Three critically-acclaimed collections of his poetry miniatures were published in Moscow and Tallinn. His *Selected Poems* appeared in Moscow in 1992. Poems included in that book have since been translated into eight languages.

Vsevolod Nekrasov was born 1934 in Moscow where he still lives. He was a member of the now famous *Lianosovo* group of poets and painters. Under the Communists, he was a *samizdat* poet, without permission to publish his work openly. His poems appeared in unofficial Russian magazines, including *37*. Since 1989 three collections of his poetry were published in Moscow and warmly received. These books, entitled *Poems from a Magazine (1989)*, *Inquiry (1991)* and *Fair and Less than Fair (1996)*, were followed by the Novosibirsk publication of his *Selected Poems (2002)*. *Ein Deutsche Buch*, a book of his essays translated into German, appeared in Bochum, also in 2002. His poems have been translated into several European languages.

Rea Nikonova (pen name of Anna Tarshis) was born in 1942 in Sverdlovsk, lived for many years in Yeisk in southern Russia, and is now based in Kiel, Germany. She started writing poetry at the end of the 1950s, and later edited several *samizdat* magazines. Her rather experimental work was published first in *samizdat* and in the Western Russian-language magazines, before it started to appear in some Russian periodicals of 1990s. Her first collection of texts entitled 'An Epigraph to Emptiness' was published in Moscow in 1997. She has since published poetry books in Germany, Canada and the US. 'Obstrugannoe Brevno Poezii', a volume of her New and Collected Poems, was published in 2002 in Spain. Gerald Janecek of Kentucky translated a number of her poems into English, and his translations have been widely anthologised.

Genrikh Sapgir (1928—1999) was born in Biysk, and lived in Moscow from early childhood. He was a member of the now famous *Lianosovo* group of poets and painters. From 1959 he published poetry for children. As for his other poems, they appeared only in émigré magazines, such as *Continent* and *Strelets/The Archer.* Since 1989 his poetry, short stories, plays and novels have been widely published in Russia. Three volumes of his *Collected Poems* appeared at the end of 1990s. He represented Russia at numerous international festivals of poetry, and his work has been published in translation throughout the world. The English translations of his *Psalms* by Jim Kates of New Hampshire have been widely anthologised and warmly received. Sapgir was the recipient of various awards including the Pushkin Prize for poetry. He is regarded by many as the most important Russian poet of the second half of the 20th century.
http://www.sapgir.narod.ru

Asya Shneiderman was born in 1968 in St. Petersburg, the only daughter of the well-known Russian painter and sculptor, Liubov Dobashina. After studying English and art at Gertsen University, St. Petersburg, she worked as a teacher of English, and now works as a librarian. Since the end of the 1990s, her poems and short stories have been published in Russian magazines and anthologies. Her first book of poems entitled *Marking Silence with a Word* was published in Moscow in 1998, and is now considered to be one of the best debut collections of the 1990s. Her translations from the Irish poet Desmond Egan appeared in his bilingual English/Russian *Selected Poems.* She is currently working on her second collection of poems.

Sergey Stratanovsky was born in 1944 in St. Petersburg. Having studied philology at St. Petersburg University, he has since worked as a librarian. He started writing poetry at the end of the 1960s; his poems have been published first in *samizdat* and in the Western Russian-language magazines. He belonged to the so-called *New Leningrad school of poetry*, which also included Joseph Brodsky, Elena Shvarts and Victor Krivulin. His first collection, simply entitled *Poems,* was published in St. Petersburg in 1993. Two critically-acclaimed books of his poems, *Daylight Darkness (2000)* and *Next to Chechnya (2002),* followed more recently. Stratanovsky is regarded by many as the most prominent St. Petersburg poet of his generation.

Alina Vitukhnovskaya was born in 1973 in Moscow, and since her youth has worked as a journalist. Having started writing poetry in the late 1980s, she published several collections of her poems, including *Anomalism (1993), The Children's Book of the Dead (1994),* and *A Romance with Fenamin (1999).* In 1990, the Russian authorities imprisoned her—allegedly for drug dealing, but, according to newspaper reports, for a refusal to become a FSB/KGB informer. At that time she had the support of most of the Russian intellectuals who protested against her unjust imprisonment and campaigned for her release. A book of her selected poems in German translation entitled *Schwarze Ikone* was published in Germany in 2002. She is regarded by many as one of the strongest 'protest' voices in contemporary Russia.
http://www.gothic.ru/alina